Zen Word, Zen Cal

ZEN WORD,
ZEN CALLIGRAPHY

Text by Eidō Tai Shimano
Calligraphy by Kōgetsu Tani

SHAMBHALA   *Boston & London*   1995

Shambhala Publications, Inc.
Horticultural Hall
300 Massachusetts Avenue
Boston, Massachusetts 02115

Published by arrangement with Theseus-Verlag AG,
Im Eigeli 4, 8700 Küsnacht, Switzerland

9   8   7   6   5   4   3   2   1

Printed in the United States of America on acid-free paper ♾
Distributed in the United States by Random House, Inc.,
and in Canada by Random House of Canada Ltd

Library of Congress Cataloging-in-Publication Data

Tani, Kōgetsu, 1931–
      [Zen Wort, Zen Schrift.   English]
      Zen word, Zen calligraphy/Kōgetsu Tani, Eidō Tai Shimano.
         p.   cm.—
      Translation of: Zen Wort, Zen Schrift.
      ISBN 1-57062-127-6 (pbk.: acid-free paper)
      1. Zen Buddhism—Terminology.   2. Calligraphy, Zen.
   I. Shimano, Eidō, 1932–   .   II. Title.
   BQ9259.5.T3613   1992   91-52518
   294.3′927—dc20   CIP

Contents

This book is dedicated to
Kajiura Itsugai Rōshi,
founder of Shōgen Junior College.

Gentle face

Wagan

This is part of the saying *wagan aigo*, "gentle face and impressive words," the most essential attitude in human relationships. This attitude can only come through years of practice of zazen and compassion.

Introduction

In Japanese, Zen words are called *zengo* and Zen calligraphies are called *bokuseki*. As you progress through this book, you will realize that *zengo* are not mere words and *bokuseki* are not mere calligraphies.

Zen words, when we read and try to understand them intellectually, very often do not seem to make any sense. Although at times they are logically presented, they may also be expressed paradoxically. This is not done as folly; the Zen masters had good reasons for expressing their messages in this way, and I have referred to this in the text as "Zen logic."

Let me give you an example. Ōbaku (d. 850) said, "In all of China, there is no Zen teacher." This initially sounds outrageous—of course there were Zen teachers in China at that time. But Ōbaku wished to make the point that Zen cannot be *taught* and used this paradoxical speech to get his point across.

It is good training to study these words and see what lies behind them and not to be deceived by superficial appearance. For example, "What is Buddha?" "Three pounds of flax." (See *Masagin.*) Yes, they are talking about flax, but at the same time they are talking about more than just flax. "Have you ever been here before?" (See *Kissako.*) It sounds like an ordinary question, but Jōshū was really asking, "Are you enlightened?" "Do you have insight?"

At first Rinzai (d. 868) was direct when he said to

his audience, "On your lump of red flesh is a true man without rank. . . ." (See *Shinnin.*) After the monk hesitated, however, Rinzai took a totally different attitude and spat out, "The true man without rank—what kind of shit-wiping stick is he!" By doing so, he presented the dynamism of True Man without Rank and transcended the categories of holy and secular. More important, with such astonishing words, he was using "shock treatment," in the hope that the monks would attain true insight. In the Zen tradition, in order to praise, a deliberately contemptuous attitude is often taken.

Think about these examples as you read the texts, and bear in mind that "things are not what they seem, nor are they otherwise." These Zen words have the most profound spirituality, but as they have been repeated over the centuries, they have lost their profundity, and only their superficial meanings remain. I have attempted in this book to break through the superficiality and reintroduce the deep meaning of *zengo* to the readers.

The calligraphies, or *bokuseki*, in this book were done by my Dharma friend Kōgetsu Tani Rōshi. There is a vast difference between calligraphers' art and Zen masters' *bokuseki*. Basically, both are done on white paper with black ink and red seals; both have good composition and both are beautiful. But, in general, calligraphers' art is not alive. *Bokuseki*, on the other hand, has life, because it is created from the *samādhi* energy of the

Zen masters' insight. Not only that, it also has breath-taking beauty and tremendous charismatic power, and it will endure through the centuries.

Until Arnold Toynbee (1889–1975) pointed out in his *History of the World* that the study of history included more than merely the Western world, few Westerners were aware of the history and tradition of the East. As a result of Toynbee's writings and World War II, the East and West became acquainted, however, and the "history of the world" at last became appreciated.

After World War II, the great exchange started: Western materialism began to move east and Zen Buddhism began to move west. In the 1960s they crossed over the Pacific and continued their migration. Zen Buddhism has gradually grown in the West, but materialism has exploded in the East. Japan is now one of the most materialistic countries in the world. Consequently, appreciation of nature, beauty, serenity, and spirituality are not considered as important as material things. Unless we wake up now, the meaning of *zengo* may fade away completely, the wisdom of the Zen masters may be forgotten, and *bokuseki* may be treated as one more material object. The intention of this book is to present the *bokuseki* and to introduce the original meaning of *zengo*. If we can appreciate *bokuseki* and *zengo* and incorporate them into our lives, we can have spiritual serenity and lucidity while living in this material world.

The seed of Zen Buddhism has sprouted in the

West. Temples and monasteries have been established, and zazen (sitting meditation) is being practiced at many centers. But the transmission of Dharma is not the physical establishment of monasteries or even zazen practice. When Zen students who are brought up in the Western thought structure and the Judeo-Christian tradition truly understand *zengo* experientially, that is when the transmission of Buddha Dharma from East to West will have been accomplished.

Easterners and Westerners must both begin to appreciate the real meaning of life. History is dramatically changing, and it is easy for us to get caught up in this fast-paced world. It is critically important for us to slow down and live each precious moment. The ancient Zen masters had it—Jakushitsu, for example (see *Hisen*). We seem to have lost it. That is why this book has been published and why it is important to read it slowly, one page a day at the most, savoring the impact of the *bokuseki,* truly absorbing the messages the masters intended in their *zengo.*

I wish to add a few technical notes. First, the characters in the original *zengo* are Chinese, not Japanese, but I have rendered the spelling according to the Japanese pronunciation. For example, if I read Rinzai's name in the Chinese style, it will be *Lin Chi,* but if I read it the Japanese way, it becomes *Rinzai.* Throughout the book I have used such Japanese pronunciations.

Second, in most of the Chinese *zengo,* the sentences

have no subject. According to the object and environment, in some cases I freely chose "I," "you," "we," or the like for the English version.

You will notice that some of the Japanese titles have two versions—*Kika Onza* and *Kike Onza*, for example. It is difficult to say which pronunciation is more accurate, but I chose the more popular one and placed it first, with the second pronunciation in parentheses.

In pronouncing many *zengo*, the sound of the vowel in one of the syllables is lengthened—*Boku Gyū*, for example. Wherever this lengthened vowel sound was necessary, it has been indicated in both the title and the text.

I would like to express my deep gratitude to Renji Ellen Darby and Sotan Heini Steinmann. Without their dedicated assistance, this book would never have been completed.

Let True Dharma continue.

Eidō Tai Shimano

Zen Word, Zen Calligraphy

牧牛図

Taming the ox
Boku Gyū

The ten oxherding scenes often pictured in Zen books illustrate the process and progress of Zen practice, using an ox as a symbol. The series begins with searching for the ox and is followed by seeing the traces, seeing the ox, and catching the ox. The fifth scene is taming the ox. This is the period in which the *un*familiar ox (our True Nature) and the familiar self get to know each other and overcome awkwardness.

Of course, each step is important, but this fifth step is just about the middle of the ten oxherding pictures. This is the turning point for the further steps: coming home on the ox's back; the ox forgotten, leaving the man alone; the ox and man both disappearing; returning to the origin; and, finally, returning to ordinary life again. *Boku gyū,* this crucial turning point, is highly significant in Zen practice.

Do nothing

Bu Ji

Bu ji is perhaps one of the most difficult Oriental thoughts to introduce to Western people. There is no equivalent in English or the European languages.

Dr. D. T. Suzuki (1870–1966) said, "This is a key term in the teaching of Rinzai. When the Dharma is truly, fully, and existentially (experientially) understood, we find there is nothing wanting in this life as we live it. Everything and anything we need is here with us and in us. One who has actually experienced this is called 'A man of *Bu Ji.*' The man of *Bu Ji* is one who has a true understanding of the Dharma or Reality and is described in Rinzai's sermon. He has an existential insight into the Self; he is the one who, being freed from externalities, is master of himself; he is a Buddha and a patriarch. He has the great business of trying to lead all his fellow beings into a state of enlightenment. He cannot remain unconcerned and indifferent so long as there is even one being left unemancipated. He works hard. He is really one of the busiest men of the world and yet he has 'no business.' "

Buddha Mind

Busshin

This is another way of saying Buddha nature or divine nature.

> Buddha mind is born in Buddha mind,
> Buddha mind grows old in Buddha mind,
> And, after all, Buddha mind dies in Buddha mind.

Because of the karmic nature of language, we have to use dualistic expressions. The truth is: Buddha mind only and nothing else. When we look at our lives from that point of view, something that is unbearable becomes bearable, something that is unforgivable may become forgivable, gratitude increases, arrogance decreases. After all, this universe is nothing but Buddha mind.

Ordinary mind
Byōjō Shin (Heijō Shin)

Jōshū (778–897) asked his teacher, Nansen (748–834), "What is the Tao?" Nansen replied, "Ordinary mind is the Tao." "Shall I try to seek after it?" Jōshū asked. "If you try for it, you will become apart from it," Nansen said. "How can I know the Tao unless I try for it?" persisted Jōshū. "The Tao is not a matter of knowing or not knowing. Knowing is delusion, not knowing is ignorance. When you have truly reached the Tao, undoubtedly you will find it as vast as the boundless space. How can it be discussed on the level of right and wrong?" With these words, it is said that Jōshū came to a sudden realization.

This dialogue is from case 19 of *Gateless Gate*. Master Mumon (1183–1260) composed a verse for it, which goes:

> In spring, hundreds of flowers,
> In summer, refreshing breeze.
> In autumn, harvest moon,
> In winter, snowflakes accompany you.
> If useless things do not hang in your mind,
> Every season is a good season.

Motivation

Dō Shin

Literally, *dō* means "way" or "Tao," and *shin* means "mind"; thus the translation is "motivation" or "quest".

There is a saying: "The way is already accomplished when one has the right motivation; the way will never be completed when one does not have the right motivation." Then what *is* the right motivation? In the Zen tradition it is expressed by four lines:

> However innumerable all beings are,
>> I vow to save them all.
> However inexhaustible delusions are,
>> I vow to extinguish them all.
> However immeasurable Dharma teachings are,
>> I vow to master them all.
> However endless the Buddha's way is,
>> I vow to follow it.

When we first chant this, it is a mere verse. Years later we may think it is contradictory. Still more years later, we recite it and practice it unconditionally. This unconditional attitude—this is *right motivation.*

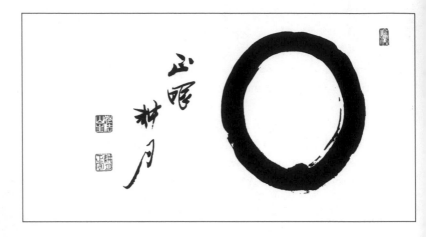

A circle

Ensō

When the Zen masters are asked to express something that is inexpressible, they often draw a circle, not necessarily a perfect round circle like one made with a compass—as a matter of fact, quite often the circles are imperfect. Sometimes a short saying is added, like, "Have a cup of tea with a round cake," or "No birth, no death." Whichever the case, the essence of this circle is the expression of *śūnyatā*, that is, nothing superfluous, nothing lacking.

Not superfluous, not deficient

En Tsū (En Zū)

Literally, *en* is the perfect circle. But the real meaning of *en* is not necessarily the circle as such—even a square, triangle, rectangle, or any other form can be called the circle from a profound Zen-spirit perspective. Regardless of the form or regardless of the spiritual, psychological, and emotional conditions, things are perfect as they are and cannot be otherwise at this moment. This is the Zen point of view.

Tsū, or *zū*, means to communicate without hindrances. Heaven and earth, men and women, are always communicating without hindrances. Without fail, a person's thoughts will reach others, whether this person is alive or deceased, whether this person is in the company of others or separated from them.

Kanzeon (Kannon) Bodhisattva is often called En Tsū Bodhisattva for these reasons.

To transmit the untransmittable

Fuden No Den

We often use the phrase "Dharma transmission." The question arises, "Transmit *what?*" Strictly speaking, "transmit *Dharma*" is not totally correct. Yet, in one instant, without speaking but with Dharma congeniality, it is quite possible to transmit this formless spirit from teacher to student. Without this transmission, no matter how many ceremonies and teachings we may learn, the teaching is not breathing life. Dharma transmission is always transmission of the untransmittable. This is the most unique part of the Rinzai Zen tradition.

福

寿海

生生

空里

虚明

耕月

Ocean of virtue
is immeasurable
Fukuju Kai Muryō

Fukuju means "fortune and longevity." *Kai* is "ocean."
Muryō is "immeasurable."

Though it may sound like an exaggeration, it is true
that the gate of virtue is wide open—"Where there is
a will, there is a way." Through our body-mind-
thought, we can cultivate karma, obtaining fortune and
longevity. "Ocean of virtue is immeasurable" is a description of the nature of Kanzeon Bodhisattva, who is
none other than our True Self. If we are not aware of
this, we must chant sutras, do prostrations, and sit
zazen until we realize our Kanzeon True Nature.

[I] know not

Fu Shiki

When the first Chinese Zen patriarch, Bodhidharma (d. 532), came from India to China, Emperor Wu (502–550) wanted to see him. The emperor asked Bodhidharma, "What is the first principle of holy teaching?" Bodhidharma said, "Vastness, not holiness." "Who is the one standing in front of me?" the emperor asked. Bodhidharma said, "I know not."

We normally think that we know many things or we believe that we can know everything. Do you know why the sun rises from the east? You may laugh and indignantly reply, "Because the planet rotates." Then let me ask you, why does the planet rotate? You may say, "It is because of Newton's second law of motion." Fine, then let me ask you further, why does such a thing as Newton's second law exist? Most likely you will say, "I don't know." This is not ignorance. Whenever we exhaust our accumulated knowledge, we speak the truth: I know not.

Cypress tree

Hakuju Shi

A monk asked Jōshū, "What is the essence of Zen Buddhism?" To this, Jōshū answered, "Cypress tree in the garden."

It sounds as though Jōshū was referring to a cypress tree in the garden as an external object, but the truth is that there are no such conditions as "external" or "internal." Jōshū *became* the cypress tree and the cypress tree *became* Jōshū.

Master Dōgen (1200–1253) said:

> To learn Buddha Dharma is to learn the self.
> To learn the self is to forget the self.
> To forget the self is to become one with
> endless dimension, Universal Mind.

When he forgot himself, Jōshū became one with the sizeless, limitless cypress tree. And it goes without saying that this spirit should apply not only to the cypress tree but to everything. This is the right attitude for Zen practice.

White cloud
Haku Un

There is a Zen expression that says:

> The blue mountain is unmoved,
> White cloud comes and goes.

This shows the contrast between blue and white, un-moved and moving, also the contrast between tangible and intangible. "Comes and goes" has a deep meaning. When Zen monks meet with their masters, they are asked, "Where are you from?" If the reply is, "I came from Kyōto," as a Zen answer it is not perfectly right. Where did we come from and where will we be going after death? This is the most fundamental question for all of us.

So "White cloud comes and goes" implies our True Being—it comes from nowhere, goes to nowhere, yet it is always floating above the blue mountain, which could be heaven, which could be hell.

Wisdom

Hannya

The word *hannya* is the transliteration of the Sanskrit term *prajñā*. The word *prajñā*, though we translate it into English as "wisdom," is best understood by the meaning of the original word.

In order to understand *prajñā*, it is useful for us to think what is *not prajñā*. Academic study is not *prajñā*, accumulation of knowledge is not *prajñā*, all acquired learning is not *prajñā*.

Prajñā, on the other hand, can be obtained through the opposite attitude, that is, by getting rid of all acquired knowledge. Mental and physical action based on instinctive intuition is *prajñā*. When one is hit, for example, one may cry, "Ouch!"—not thinking good or bad, just universal "Ouch!" This is *prajñā*.

Ceaseless daily practice
Heiso Ni Ari

Every single day's practice of mindfulness permeates one's entire body and is thus revealed in one's behavior. When days pass without any problems, the results of the accumulation of such practice may not be revealed so drastically, but when unexpected, extraordinary things happen, one's everyday practice and everyday mindfulness arise spontaneously and accordingly. Since life, in general, is unpredictable, we need to prepare to meet these unpredictable happenings. Hence, it is extremely important for us to continue daily practice.

Light
Hikari

There is a beautiful Pali verse that goes:

> Dwell!
> You are the Light itself.
> Rely on yourself,
> Do not rely on others.
> The Dharma is the Light,
> Rely on the Dharma.
> Do not rely on anything other than Dharma.

We normally think of light as coming from the sun. Light also comes from the moon, the stars, candles, and fire. From the Zen Buddhist point of view, however, the most important light is the internal light, or, to be more precise, we are the light itself, nothing else. The light just shines. "Endless Dimension Universal Light" is another name for Amitābha Buddha and is a poetic expression of our True Nature.

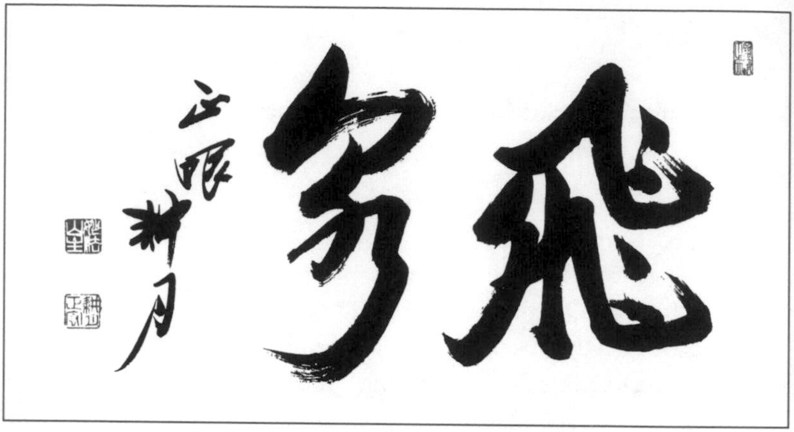

Waterfall

Hisen

Hisen literally means "flying springs," the poetic expression of waterfall. These rather unique words came from a poem by Jakushitsu (1290–1367), which goes:

> The wind tousles the flying springs
> That makes the cool sound.
> From the peak of the mountain
> The moon rises and the bamboo
> Window is reflected brightly.
> In my old age I especially feel that
> Living in the deep mountains is desirable.
> If I die at the foot of this mountain rock,
> Even my bones must be pure.

The last line, "Even my bones must be pure," is especially well known because it is an unprecedented expression. Some people think that ashes are not pure, but with zazen and a regulated life in the deep mountains, our souls become pure—why not our bones?

Unprecedented, unrepeatable encounter

Ichigo Ichie

Ii Naosuke (1815–1860) was chief administrator of the Tokugawa Shōgunate and was also a tea master. Because of the radical change he instituted, he had many enemies and was constantly threatened with assassination.

Every day, before he left for the castle, he made a bowl of tea by himself, saying that it was an unprecedented tea and, most likely, an unrepeatable tea. Thus he practiced tea meditation.

One snowy morning in the spring of 1860, he was assasinated; however, this saying, *Ichigo ichie*, lived on, and now it is the most important motto for the Zen tea students.

A day of no work
is a day of no eating
Ichinichi Nasazareba Ichinichi Kurawazu

This motto used in Zen monasteries was said by Hya-kujō Ekai (720–814). This story goes as follows.

Master Hyakujō was working outside every day (an activity that Zen Buddhist monks calls *samu*). He was quite aged, so his students asked him not to work. But Hyakujō ignored their suggestion and continued to work every day. So a monk hid his mattock; thus Hyakujō could not work. As a result, Hyakujō went into his room and sat quietly. The attendant brought him three meals a day. Hyakujō did not eat them. No matter how many times the attendant begged him to eat, Hyakujō refused. The attendant monk asked, "Master, what's the matter with you?" To this Hyakujō replied, "A day of no work is a day of no eating."

Work does not only mean in the fields. Zazen is one of the most important works in our tradition. So we can say: A day of no zazen is a day of no eating.

真
眼視
象生
二醒
更耕
月

Seeing all sentient beings with compassionate eyes

Jigen Ji Shujō

This phrase appears in the twenty-fifth chapter of the *Lotus Sūtra:* Kanzeon Bodhisattva sees all sentient beings with the eyes of compassion.

One of the differences between Buddhism and Christianity is that in Christianity there is one God. In Buddhism there are many Buddhas and Bodhisattvas, and with their combined efforts, they help deluded beings. Kanzeon Bodhisattva is one of those whose specialty is said to be compassion.

Let me ask you: Who is and where is Kanzeon Bodhisattva?

Eternal, joyous,
selfless, and pure

Jō Raku Ga Jō

Jō raku ga jō is from *Enmei Jukku Kannon Gyō*, the ten-phrase life-prolonging *Kannon Sūtra*, which is chanted every morning in Zen monasteries. "Eternal, joyous, selfless, and pure" are the descriptions of our True Nature. Though unenlightened people think that life is finite, it isn't. They think that life is painful, but it isn't. They think that we are selfish, but we aren't. They think that life is defiled, but it isn't. This sūtra is pointing to the essential reality of our True Nature, while unenlightened people are talking about and believing in a deluded reality. To chant this sutra leads us to realize eternity, joy, selflessness, and purity.

Barrier

Kan

When the founder of Myoshin-ji (a compound of temples and a monastery), Kanzan Egen (1277–1360), visited his teacher, Shūhō Myōchō (1282–1338) at the age of fifty-four, he was asked to work on *Kan*, a well-known Zen kōan of Unmon (864–949). Egen worked day and night, sat and sat in zazen intensively. At last he broke through his inner barrier. All of a sudden he realized his own True Nature. With congratulations, Shūhō Myōchō gave him the Dharma name Kanzan.

We have so many barriers in our hearts and minds. Because of these countless barriers, we make ourselves slaves. Zen practice is nothing other than being free from spiritual slavery.

Sitting quietly

Kan Za

Kan is an interesting Chinese character that consists of a temple gate and one tree. Try to visualize one huge tree standing alone within the boundary of the temple grounds. That image itself gives us the profound serenity and quietness that are not mere soundlessness or voicelessness. *Za* is sitting. So *Kan za* may be translated as "quiet sitting," as in zazen, when one becomes like a gigantic tree with deep roots inhaling heavenly oxygen and exhaling it to the center of the earth.

In this day and age, more than anything *kan za* time is needed—it gives our lives serenity and spiritual contentedness.

夏云多奇峰山底耕月

Summer clouds appear in many strange forms

Kaun Kihō Ōshi

Compared with other seasons, summer has particularly unique cloud formations. If we watch them closely for even one minute, we are surprised at how much change can occur within only sixty seconds.

Impermanency is not theory but dynamic fact. Creation, creation, change, change. It is the summer sky that shows us this silent drama, and it is up to us whether we view these clouds as merely strange forms or understand them as dynamic impermanence. The sky doesn't tell us but silently and openly shows us the dramatic Dharma.

Returning to original home
Kika Onza (*Kike Onza*)

As in the ten oxherding pictures (see *Boku Gyū*), we start from ignorance (yet with motivation). After years of practice, with the readiness of time, we come to the point where both person and ox have disappeared (essentially, not a "thing" exists). This is an indispensable experience, but it is not the goal.

The goal, if any, is to return once more to ordinary life and, in the midst of human defilement, to sit and to work without being defiled, without being disturbed. As Rinzai says:

> You have only to be ordinary with nothing to *do*.
> Defecating, urinating, putting on clothes, eating
> food, lying down when tired. Fools laugh at me,
> but the wise man understands.

Have a cup of tea
Kissako

During the T'ang dynasty in China there lived an out-standing Zen master, Jōshū. One day a traveling monk came to see him. Jōshū asked, "Have you ever been here before?" The monk replied, "Yes, I have." Jōshū said, "Have a cup of tea."

Another traveling monk came to see Jōshū. Jōshū asked, "Have you ever been here before?" The monk said, "No." Jōshū said, "Have a cup of tea."

Jōshū's attendant monk, who was present on the two occasions, was rather puzzled and asked his master, "Why did you say, 'Have a cup of tea' to a monk who has achieved insight and then say, 'Have a cup of tea' to a monk who is still blind in Dharma?" Jōshū said, "Have a cup of tea."

It goes without saying that this is Jōshū's Zen, transcending intellectualization, just "Have a cup of tea." That's it! This tea is universal tea. To taste this tea is to taste Zen. To say this is even too much perhaps.

太拳

廿三路

辛未神月

There is only one way
Kokon Muni No Michi

The literal definition of *kokon* is "past and present," that is, from beginningless beginning to endless end. *Muni no michi* is one way, not two or three ways. This Dharma, incomparably profound and minutely subtle—this way is the only one in the past, present, and future.

The Japanese haiku poet Bashō (1644–1694) said,

> Along this Way
> Goes no one
> This autumn evening

This is the only way for him.

心

如秋碧月

留痕耕月

禅正院

[My] mind is like
an autumn moon
Kokoro Shūgetsu Ni Nitari

This phrase is taken from a well-known Chinese poem:

My mind is like an autumn moon,
Pure and transcendentally elegant.
It is impossible to compare this mind with anything.
How could it be possible for me to explain it to you?

How could it be possible for me to explain it to *you*? But just to avoid misunderstanding, let me say that "my mind" does not mean egoistical mind. It is another way of saying that everybody's Buddha nature is like an autumn moon, lucid and pure—nothing can be compared to it.

Zen practice is, after all, to realize this wonderful True Nature.

[Temple of] Diamond, [Temple of] True Dharma Eye glitter in heaven and earth

Kongō Shōgen Kenkon Ni Kagayaku

This is a traditional saying, yet it is almost a karmic coincidence that the authors of this book represent both the Diamond and the True Dharma Eye. Kōgetsu Tani Rōshi is the abbot of Shōgen-ji, Temple of True Dharma Eye, and Eidō Tai Shimano Rōshi is the abbot of Kongō-ji, Temple of the Diamond.

It goes without saying that not only these temples but all temples, even a speck of dust, are always glittering. However, through interesting karmic events, these two temples have developed a strong Dharma link. Sangha relations have also been firmly established, shining in heaven and earth.

Let True Dharma continue, universal Sangha relations, International Dai Bosatsu Zendōs everywhere become complete!

What is this?

Kore Nanzo

Master Bassui (1327–1387) said in a Dharma talk, "If you want to free yourself of the sufferings of the six realms, you must learn the direct way to become a Buddha. This way is no other than the realization of your own Mind." He continued, "If you want to realize your own Mind, you must first of all look into the source from which thoughts flow. Sleeping and working, standing and sitting, profoundly ask yourself, 'What is this?'"

"What is this?" is another way of saying, "Who am I?"—the greatest question of human life! Many of us do not even realize how important this question is. In Zen Buddhism, however, to know one's own True Self is the quintessential question, and self-realization is the "goal."

Master Bassui cautioned us, however, saying, "Upon such realization, question yourself even more intensely in this way: My body is like a phantom, like bubbles on a stream. My mind, looking into itself, is as formless as empty space, yet somewhere within, sounds are perceived. Who is hearing?"

What is this?

Shout

Kwatzu

Master Rinzai said, "Sometimes a shout is like the jeweled sword of the Vajra King; sometimes a shout is like the golden-haired lion crouching on the ground; sometimes a shout is like a whip-tipped fishing pole; sometimes a shout does not function as a shout."

Though all shouts are just *kwatzu*, each one is different. When the man of Dharma shouts "*Kwatzu!*" with brisk spirit, his *kwatzu* is like the jeweled sword of the Vajra King. But what does it mean to say, "Sometimes a shout does not function as a shout"? This may be called "shoutless shout" or "silent shout," the complete manifestation of Rinzai himself, the best shout of the four categories.

Rationally speaking, this may not make sense. Although Zen is not anti-intellect, the profound Zen spirit cannot be grasped by logic and a rational way of thinking. The real is not rational. If Zen were more intellectual and rational, it would have died out centuries ago.

写佛心经

Watch your step
Kyakka O Miyo

At the entrance of most Zen monasteries, there is a plaque that reads, "Watch your step." Superficially, it is a suggestion: Be careful, watch where you are walking.

But the real meaning of "Watch your step" is that in your everyday activities, both physical and mental, you should be ceaselessly mindful.

A monk asked Master Kakumyō (1271–1361), "What is the essence of Zen?" Master Kakumyō replied, "Watch your step."

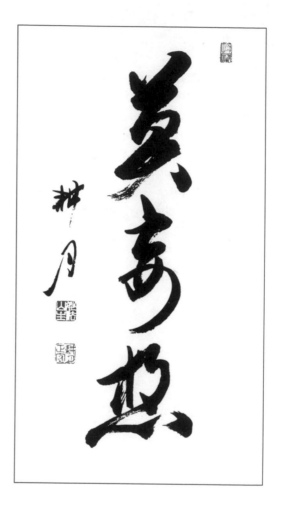

Don't be deluded

Maku Mōzō

Master Mugō (760–821), whenever asked a question by anyone, answered only, "Don't be deluded."

To say "Buddha," to think "Dharma," to speak about "Ultimate Reality," are all considered delusion. Master Mugō's teaching was just "Don't be deluded." The essence of *Maku mōzō*, however, with no translation even necessary, is the direct presentation of the Unspeakable Reality.

Three pounds of flax

Masagin

A monk asked Master Tōzan (910–990), "What is Buddha?" Tōzan replied, "Three pounds of flax."

"What is Buddha?" is a simple question yet a deep question. In the ancient days of China, disciples often asked their teachers, "What is Buddha?" Different teachers responded in different ways. In this case, Tōzan said, "Three pounds of flax." Similar to "Cypress tree in the garden" by Jōshū (see *Hakuju Shi*), questioner and answerer become one. When this unification happens, such an answer comes forth instantaneously and with great impact.

明

晴隻々

山眠耕月

Light and darkness
are intermingled

Meian Sōsō

In light, objects are visible; therefore, all phenomena such as big and small, black and white, young and old, can be distinguished. This may be called the realm of relativity.

In darkness, on the other hand, objects are invisible to the eye; hence, no distinction is possible. This may be called the realm of sameness.

Sōsō literally means "intermingled"; therefore, the total meaning is: there is relativity in sameness and sameness in relativity.

As far as Buddha nature is concerned, we are all the same. As far as personality is concerned, we are all different. In modern days, equality, or sameness, has become popular, but the traditional saying goes:

> Equality without clear distinction
> is not the teaching of Buddha Dharma.
> Distinction without absolute equality
> is not the teaching of Buddha Dharma either.

Let us appreciate this saying.

Clearly revealed as it is
Mei Rekireki Ro Dōdō

Confucius (551–479 B.C.E.) said, "I have nothing to hide." To say it more clearly, there is nothing that is hidden; everything is revealed as it is.

The sound of peaceful music, the sound of terrible noise, are both clearly revealed as they are and nothing else. Nonetheless, we prefer the peacefulness and dislike the irritation of the noise. We try to control, to change things to how we want them. This can be done to a certain degree but cannot be done completely and eternally. If, on the other hand, we accept things as they are and see things as clearly revealed as they are, that acceptance itself is the first step toward unbreakable peacefulness.

源遠流深

虚窗耕月

耕山主人

With sufficient depth,
spring will amply supply stream
Minamoto Fukakareba Nagare Tōshi

As in many other cases, this saying may give readers the impression that it is speaking about "spring" and "stream" in the literal sense. Zen writing traditionally uses symbolism, however, and this is not an exception.

The real meaning of this saying is that when there is profound practice and sufficient study is accomplished, one can teach endlessly and influence innumerable people. Nowadays, instant results are popular and people are often impatient. Even so, people realize that the classics—art, music, literature—have endured for centuries because of their depth.

東去

正峰
耕月

Not yet
Mi Zai

Hakuun Shutan (1025–1072) said, "A few Zen students have come from a distant place. They are all enlightened. They preach well, their knowledge of Buddhist philosophy is wide and deep, and when I asked them to compose a poem, they did it very well. But they are 'not yet.'" This is the origin of the well-known saying "Not yet."

When we think about our study and practice, there is no end, no graduation, "not yet." Nevertheless, we are goal-oriented and therefore expect completion. Zen students consider even "completion" as "not yet." We walk this path endlessly and each step is *it*, yet "not yet," yet this is *it*.

狗

月明松下房栊静
日出雲中雞犬喧

笑山人耕月

泰

日出雲中雞犬喧

笑山人耕月

Scoop up the water,
the moon is in your hands
Mizu O Kiku Sureba, Tsuki Te Ni Ari

Toy with the flowers and their
fragrance scents your garments
Hana O Rō Sureba, Ka E Ni Mitsu

These two lines are by Kidō Chigu (1185–1269). When we scoop up water, the moon is in our hands; at the same time, it is in the sky. When we toy with the flowers, their fragrance permeates our garments. "I enter into you and you enter into me," as the saying goes.

Because of the poetic expression of perfect infusion, we may miss the point, so let me remind you that the point is: to scoop and to toy. To scoop and to toy are the deeds and are none other than the practice. Only through scooping and toying can moon and hand become one and fragrance and garment become truly inseparable.

Silence

Moku

In the *Vimalakīrti Sūtra*, one of the most dramatized of Mahāyāna literature, Vimalakīrti was asked by Mañjuśrī Bodhisattva about the essence of the Buddhist teaching. Vimalakīrti kept silent. Someone commented that Vimalakīrti's silence was like thunder.

When we read Zen texts, we often see such expressions as "The monk kept silent." There are at least three different kinds of silence. First, the monk does not know what to say, out of ignorance. Second, he pretends that he is ignorant, yet his true intention is to see the reaction of the Dharma opponent. The third case is that of an enlightened monk who knows that *this matter* cannot be explained, hence silence. The third silence is like thunder.

Nothing

Mu

A monk asked Jōshū, "Has a dog Buddha nature or not?" Jōshū replied, "*Mu.*"

Mumon, the compiler of *Gateless Gate*, said in his comments, "Employ every ounce of your energy to work on this *Mu*. If you hold on without interruption, behold: a single spark and the holy candle is lit!"

He also said, "In order to master Zen, you must pass the barrier of the patriarchs. To attain this subtle realization, you must completely cut off the way of thinking. What is the barrier of the patriarchs? It is the single word, *Mu*. That is the front gate to Zen."

In the Rinzai Zen tradition, students are forced to concentrate their total being into this *Mu*, become *Mu*, nothing but *Mu*, *Mu*, *Mu*. Suddenly they see the dynamism of *Mu* in their lives and the lives of all creatures. Not only that, the fundamental question of life and death will also become clear. *Mu* is a label pasted on our True Nature.

Literally, *Mu* means "nothing." Truly it is nothing. We are deceived by many tangible "existences" and think that they exist. But, after all, there is nothing, *no* thing.

Selflessness

Mu Ga

People may interpret selflessness as a moral and ethical term. In a way it is a beautiful attitude to be selfless, but Zen Buddhism is not talking about this kind of attitude, rather about realizing the Fundamental Reality that has no self, no entity, no element, and no particles. Rather, this endless dimensioned universe is the self itself.

Not a "thing" exists

Muichimotsu

When the sixth patriarch, Enō Daikan (638–713), was still an unknown layman under the fifth patriarch, Gunin Daiman (601–674), it is said that the fifth patriarch wanted to select his Dharma heir and asked his disciples to compose a Zen verse. Responding to this, the layman Enō wrote the following verse on the wall:

> Salvation is nothing like a tree,
> Nor a clear mirror;
> Essetially, not a "thing" exists;
> What is there then for the dust to fall on?

Because of this, the record says, Enō was later appointed to become the sixth patriarch.

"Essentially, not a 'thing' exists" is a very hard statement to accept, because it looks as though we really exist, a table exists, a mountain exists; but when a true insight experience takes place, not a "thing" exists and at that time we understand that what we believed to be real is, in fact, like a dream and a fantasy. With this understanding we eliminate unnecessary pain caused by delusion. Indeed, not a "thing" exists.

Inexhaustibility

Mujinzō

The saying goes:

> Within nothingness, there is inexhaustibility.
> Look, there is a flower, there is the moon, there is a
> pagoda.

It is easy for us to understand the second part of this saying, but what about the first part?

According to "Zen logic," because there is fundamentally nothing, inexhaustible things can be revealed. Zen logic, by nature, refuses intellectual interpretation. If, however, we attempt to interpret intellectually we come to the conclusion that nothingness and inexhaustibility are incompatible.

In the same way, you can say that Zen logic is confusing: "exists yet does not exist, does not exist yet exists." What makes sense superficially does not, in fact, make any sense. What does not make sense superficially is that which does make sense.

No merit whatsoever, no virtue at all

Mukudoku

When Bodhidharma, the first patriarch of Zen in China, came from India, Emperor Wu said to him, "I am a faithful Buddhist, I built many temples, printed sūtra books, and made offerings to the monks. What kind of merit will I get?" To this, Bodhidharma answered, "No merit whatsoever, no virtue at all."

We have a tendency to do something with the expectation that we will be compensated. There is a doer and there is a receiver, and in between there is compensation. But in the world of oneness, there is no giver, no receiver, no donation. There is just pure doing and therefore no expectation and no disappointment. When we come to this understanding, we know the true meaning of "No merit whatsoever, no virtue at all."

Holding a flower
Nenge

When Buddha was in the Ryoju Mountains, he turned a flower in his fingers and presented it in front of the audience. Everyone kept silent. Only the head disciple, Mahākāśyapa, smiled. Buddha said, "I have the eyes of the True Dharma, the subtle mind of nirvāna, the true form of no-form. This Dharma is beyond words, but I now declare that the spirit of this Dharma has been transmitted to Mahākāśyapa." This was the beginning of the Dharma transmission from Śākyamuni Buddha to his disciples.

Nenge means "holding a flower." "Holding a flower" shows Buddha's appreciation of it; he and the flower became one. Observing this, Mahākāśyapa smiled in appreciation of this oneness. Mumon, in his cynical comment, asked, "If everyone in the audience had smiled, how could Śākyamuni Buddha have transmitted the Dharma? If Mahākāśyapa had not smiled, how could the Buddha have transmitted the Dharma?" After all, it is just holding a flower, nothing more, nothing less. A great Zen saying goes: "Just do it!"

念念不离心

随心记
出离月

Each *nen* comes from the Mind
Each *nen* is not apart from the Mind

Nen Nen Jū Shin Ki
Nen Nen Fū Ri Shin

Nen, existentially speaking, can be translated as "thought." When fundamentally interpreted, it is Mind itself. To illustrate this phrase, it is best to think of the image of water and wave. Water is Mind, wave is thought. Thoughts arise from the Mind, yet at the same time thoughts are still a part of the Mind, inseparable yet clearly distinguished, nondualistic yet seemingly two. If we understand this reality, there is no thought that may be disliked, and there is no thought that is preferred.

Nen nen jū shin ki. Nen nen fū ri shin. These are the last two lines from *Enmei Jukku Kannon Gyō*, the ten-phrase life-prolonging *Kannon Sūtra*, which is frequently chanted in the Zen tradition.

日日是好日
一眠耕月

Every day is a good day
Nichi Nichi Kore Kōjitsu

Master Unmon said to his disciples, "I do not ask anything about your spiritual condition before the fifteenth day of the month, but tell me something about it after the fifteenth day of the month." Nobody answered. So Master Unmon gave the answer for us all: "Every day is a good day." On the fifteenth day of the month, according to the lunar calendar, there is a full moon, which implies clear enlightenment. "After the fifteenth day of the month" means after such realization.

As for "Every day is a good day," many are deceived by "good" and think that good is the opposite of bad. Thus, many think that "good day" means happy, beautiful day. Unmon, however, did not mean it that way. Unmon's "good day" is far more profound. He was pointing to right here, right now, unprecedented, unrepeatable, absolute day. A good kōan for us all is: "What kind of day is this?"

Patience

Nin

Nyōgen Senzaki (1876-1958) wrote the following poem in Chinese in reference to his teacher, Sōen Shaku (1859–1919):

> How can I forget his angry face?
> How can I forget the blows of his strong fist?
> Thirty years in America
> I worked my way to answer him—
> Cultivating a Buddhist field in this strange land.
> This autumn, the same as in the past,
> I have no crop but the growth of my white hair.
> The wind whistles like his scolding voice,
> And the rain hits me,
> Each drop like his whip.
> Hey!

Senzaki, despite his burning love of Zen and desire to transmit it to the West, waited seventeen years after arriving in America before beginning to teach, in order to follow the instructions of his teacher.

What better example of patience can be given than this? And what better rewards of patience can be shown than Senzaki's ultimate influence on American Zen students?

心如

As if one is still here

Owasu Ga Gotoshi (Nyo Zai)

Even after a person has passed away, we often feel as if that person is still with us; or, when someone goes away for many years, if the person has a strong influence, he is not forgotten.

The feeling of existence is none other than one's degree of karmic energy. When karmic energy is strong, whether it is good or bad, the person's influence or teaching continues. On the contrary, if a person has weak karmic energy, this person is easily forgotten. Karmic energy is something that we can cultivate through zazen practice. Śākyamuni Buddha, for example, is still alive.

Transcend the duality
Ryō Bō (Ryō Mō)

There is a saying by a Chinese scholar: "It is best to transcend both internal and external." When one can transcend both, the mind is lucid and calm. *Ryō bō* literally means "forget both." "Both" means such things as in and out, life and death. We call these duality or dualism. The point of Zen practice is to be free from phenomenal dualism and reach a level where there is no dualism, not even monism. We can name things under "ism" like Buddhism, nationalism, Communism, but we cannot practice "ism." When one comes to the essential point, one is not even aware that one has transcended. This condition is called *Ryō bō.*

水流心不競

雲在意俱遲

山暗耕月

Flowing streams do not compete with one another

Ryūsui Saki O Arasowazu

This saying is a saying of naturalness. The streams do not say, "Go ahead" or "After you." They flow naturally, just naturally. But when we look at human life, there is much competition and there are many competitive dramas, so this phrase is a teaching of how important it is for us to be natural.

There is a similar saying in the Zen tradition that goes:

> However quick the stream may be,
> It does not carry away the reflection of the moon.

Water is water, moon is moon, well balanced and in tune with one another—that is nature.

Planting the pine

Saishō

In the *Rinzai Roku* ("Recorded Sayings of Rinzai"), there is a story that goes: "When Rinzai was planting pine trees, his teacher, Ōbaku, asked, 'What's the good of planting so many trees in the deep mountains?' Rinzai replied, 'First, I want to make a natural setting for the main gate; second, I want to make a landmark for later generations.' Rinzai then thumped the ground three times with his mattock and breathed out a great breath. Understanding this, Ōbaku said, 'Under you my line will flourish throughout the world.'"

Because of this historical event, even nowadays most Rinzai Zen monasteries plant a pine tree on Rinzai's Day, wishing to make a beautiful natural setting for the main gate and also to make a landmark for the generations to come.

Let True Dharma continue.

No calendar in the mountain monastery

Sanchū Rekijitsu Nashi

This is the ideal condition of a mountain monastery, where only the sun and moon rise and set. When spring comes, flowers bloom, and when winter comes, snow-flakes fall. There is no January, February, no Saturday, Sunday. Life goes with nature—no schedules, no appointments. When visitors come, they just come—no planning, no cancellations, just coming and going with nature. *Sanchū rekijitsu nashi.*

Blooming mountain flowers are like golden brocade

Sanka Hiraite Nishki Ni Nitari

A monk asked the Chinese master Dairyō (who was descended in the Dharma lineage from Tokusan, but not much is known about him), "The physical body decomposes; what is the indestructible Dharma body?" To this Master Dairyō responded with a verse that goes:

> Blooming mountain flowers are like golden brocade,
> Brimming mountain waters are blue as indigo.

In Zen literature, a traveling monk often asks about Dharma body, that is, what is Dharma? To this question, hundreds of different responses have been recorded, but "Blooming mountain flowers are like golden brocade" is one of the best known.

As always, this response gives the impression that Master Dairyō was describing external beauty. Yes, his reply is a description of external beauty, but more than that, it is an expression "transcending words."

[Endlessly talking about the feeling of] mountains, clouds, oceans, and moon
San Un Kai Getsu

Human conversation depends on language. After talking for a certain period of time, either we are tired or the subject of the conversation becomes exhausted. But when we look at a flower and can converse with this flower, communication can be endlessly long and extremely subtle. Especially when we talk with wildflowers, we rediscover how significant a seemingly insignificant flower may be.

In Zen Buddhism we don't believe in the existence of God in the way the Judeo-Christian tradition does. But when we communicate with the solid mountain, floating cloud, vast ocean, and beautiful moon, we can't help but feel that there must be "something" that created all of these.

Pure wind, clear moon

Seifū Meigetsu

Imagine you are looking up at the full moon on an autumn night, a cool breeze gently caressing your face with a silken touch—no noise—not hot, not cold.

Master Hakuin (1686–1769) said in his *Song of Zazen:*

> How boundless the cleared sky of *samādhi!*
> How transparent the perfect moonlight of
> the Fourfold Wisdom!
> At this moment what more need we seek?
> As the Truth eternally reveals itself,
> This very place is the Lotus Land of Purity,
> This very body is the Body of the Buddha.

What more need we say?

Snow, moon, flower
Setsu Gekka (Setsu Getsu Ka)

Master Dōgen composed a poem that goes:

> In spring, a flower blooms,
> In summer, a cuckoo cries,
> In autumn, a beautiful moon,
> And in winter, snowfall and coolness revealed.

The key words of this poem is not "flower," not "moon," not "snowfall," but it is "coolness." Dōgen is pointing to cool mind, cool life.

However, snow, moon, and flower are representative of seasons, and with snow, Zen people say, the universe falls, with moon the universe shines, with flower the universe blooms. This is "coolness."

My teacher, Sōen Rōshi (1907–1984), wrote a haiku poem that goes:

> Mountain coolness
> Dharma net
> Now spread East and West!

心

如月法

正眼耕月

There is no Dharma apart from Mind

Shinge Muhō

There is a saying: "The triple world is but one Mind." Outside the Mind there is no other reality; Mind, Buddha, all sentient creatures—these three are not different. The "triple world" here means the material world, the world of sensuous desire and the formless, immaterial, spiritual world. Whatever the case, from the Zen point of view, there is nothing but Mind. Blue mountain is Mind, floating white cloud is also Mind. Only one mind.

True man [without rank]

Shinnin

In the *Rinzai Roku*, there is a dialogue that goes, "The Master took the high seat in the hall. He said, 'On your lump of red flesh is a true man without rank who is always going in and out of the face of every one of you. Those of you who have not yet proved him, look, look!' Then a monk came forward and asked, 'What about the true man without rank?' The Master got down from his seat, seized the monk, and cried, 'Speak, speak!' The monk faltered. Shoving him away, the Master said, 'The true man without rank—what kind of shit-wiping stick is he!' Then he returned to his quarters."

Needless to say, "true man" does not mean man as a human being. The best way to say it is that the true man is an unnameable something without category that doesn't need to practice, that doesn't seek self-realization. Everyone, whether we know it or not, is such a person fundamentally.

Words sound beautiful and elegant, but they lack dynamism. Rinzai wanted to point out that our rankless, boundless, vast nature is brisk, is alive and acts dynamically. He thus presented us with the essence of Rinzai Zen.

Think about distant future

Shi On

There is a poem composed by my teacher, Sōen Nakagawa Rōshi. When I first met him in 1954, he gave it to
me. I was very moved by it and, even now, deeply in-
volved in Dharma activity in the West, the poem, especially the last two lines, continues to be my constant
inspiration.

> Wearing black robe and straw sandals,
> I walk soundlessly.
> Thinking of the far distant future, my eyes never
> cease to gaze toward the ultimate reality.

Let True Dharma continue

Shōbō Kujū

"Let True Dharma continue" is a prayer. However, whether we pray or not, the Dharma *will* continue. The creation of heaven and earth was Dharma; the continuation of heaven and earth is also Dharma. No heaven, no earth is Dharma too. So in that sense it is unnecessary to pray, unnecessary to even call it "True Dharma."

But True Dharma, which has been transmitted from Śākyamuni Buddha, through all the patriarchs to the present masters, must continue to be transmitted, generation after generation, east to west, north to south. That requires intense prayer and dedication. Otherwise, this teaching and tradition will become extinct. For this reason, every day we chant, "Let True Dharma continue."

生死和一眼

山亭秋月

No life, no death
Shōji Nashi

Kanzan Egen is the founder of Shōgen-ji and Myōshin-ji. He greatly influenced his disciples but did not leave any recorded sayings. After Egen's physical departure, Ingen (1592–1673), of the Ōbaku school, came from China and visited Myōshin-ji. He paid his respects to the founder's grave and asked the priest, "Did your founder leave any recorded sayings?" "No, he did not." "What!" Ingen cried. "If he did not leave any recorded sayings, Myōshin-ji is not worthy of recognition." The priest was frightened but reluctantly said, "Though our founder did not leave any recorded sayings, I heard that he said, 'The kōan of the Cypress Tree has depriving power and Egen has no life, no death.'" Upon hearing these words from the priest, Ingen was impressed and said, "Very good," bowed deeply, and left Myōshin-ji.

A modern Zen master, when he was going to die, said, "Now I die to live forever." Buddha nature has no life and no death.

The pines grew old
and the clouds idled

Shō Rō Un Kan

In the preface to the *Rinzai Roku*, Babo (twelfth century) said:

> As the pines grew old and the clouds idled
> He found boundless contentment within himself.

Having practiced many decades, at last Master Rinzai dwelled in a place where he found boundless contentment within himself. In this day and age what more need we seek?

秋

月揚明輝

山居秋月

Autumn moon is especially brilliant and clear

Shūgetsu Myōki O Agu

Autumn moon on the lunar calendar is called Jūgoya in Japanese. This is approximately September 15 according to the Gregorian calendar. Every month throughout the year there is a full moon—why is Jūgoya so special?

It has been said that during autumn, the sky becomes clearer than during the rest of the seasons and the moon shines particularly brightly. Quite often we read of this kind of impression, and the poet, though talking about the moon, is also speaking about more than the moon. He is pointing out our own True Nature, which is not given by anyone else and cannot be taken away by anyone else. It is eternally lucid and brilliant.

春風河上柳
夜雨潤田澤

Spring water fills the
rivers in four directions
Shun Sui Shitaku Ni Mitsu

When spring comes, ice and snow melt, and rivers filled with spring waters run in four directions: north, south, east, and west.

The implication of this saying is that after one obtains self-realization, self-confidence, and self-reliance, the negative ice and doubtful snow melt, and one can offer oneself to others.

Kenji Miyazawa (1896–1933) said in a poem:

> If in the east there's a sick child,
> going and nursing him.
> If in the west there's a tired mother,
> going and carrying for her bundles of rice.
> If in the south there's someone dying,
> going and saying you don't have to be afraid.
> If in the north there's a quarrel or a lawsuit,
> saying it's not worthy, stop it.
> In a drought, shedding tears,
> in a cold summer, pacing back and forth, lost,
> called a good-for-nothing by everyone,
> neither praised
> nor thought a pain.
> Someone like that
> is what I want to be.

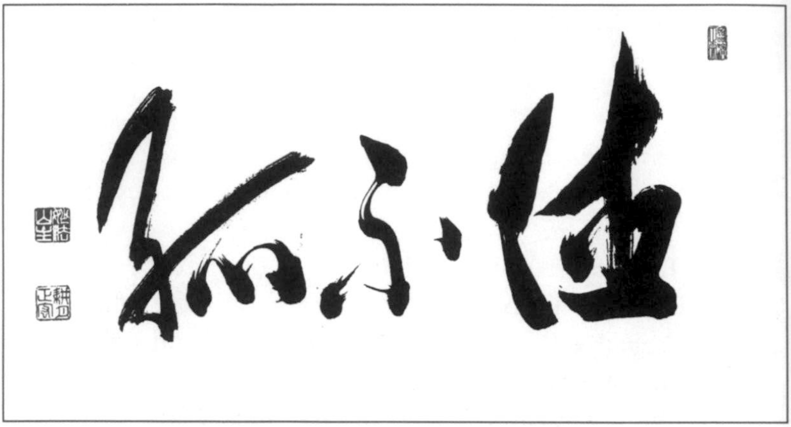

The man of vitrue is not alone
Toku Wa Ko Narazu

The phrase "The man of virtue is not alone" is not clear, because this is only half of the verse from the *Analects of Confucius*. The second half goes, "Always there is someone who helps."

The original term for virtue is *toku,* and this is one of those words for which an equivalent cannot be found in European languages. *Toku* is a good act inconspicuously done, a good thought unrewarded, or a good deed uncompensated. And that *toku* accumulates and transmits through the generations. In East Asian thought there are such things as *toku* from previous lives or receiving one's parents' *toku*. Like karma, or like the law of conservation of energy in physics, *toku* is never lost. A person of *toku* is one who is often called "lucky guy" or "lucky girl," but it is not mere luck; it is the result of inevitability.

天嶺秀孤松正眠耕月

Winter mountain, solitary pine is conspicuous

Tōrei Koshō Hiizu

Because of the snow, winter mountains are white. Owing to the evergreen's nature, the pine needles are green. In this case, only one pine tree is standing alone on the white mountain.

A monk asked Master Hyakujō, "What is the most wonderful thing in our lives?" Hyakujō, replied, "I am sitting alone on this sublime peak." "Alone" does not mean exclusively—I'm sitting here with a flower, with the moon, with snow, with an animal, with universal Sangha. The monk bowed as though to say, "Thank you for your teaching." Hyakujō hit him as the finishing touch to the Dharma battle.

The solitary pine stands alone, not exclusively but with universal Sangha.

Though the moon sets,
it never leaves the universe

Tsuki Ochite Ten O Hanarezu

Sunrise, sunset. Moonrise, moonset. Every day we think that the moon literally disappears, but we know that it will come back again. When someone dies, it is thought that that person disappears, but it is impossible to disappear from endless dimension, universal world.

Ōbaku said:

> Mind is like a vast space in which there is no good or evil, as when the sun shines upon the four corners of the world. For when the sun rises and illuminates the whole earth, the vast space does not get brighter; and when the sun sets, the universe does not get dark. The phenomena of light and dark alternate with each other, but the nature of the universe is unchanged. The same is true with the Mind of the Buddha and of sentient beings.

Training monk

Unsui

Literally, *un* means cloud, *sui* means water. Like clouds, like water, truth seekers gather and dwell at certain places and form the Sangha. At the same time, like clouds, like water, they float from one place to another. Therefore, *unsui* means monk-in-training. In the Rinzai tradition, it is a requirement that all monks go to a Zen monastery as *unsui* and receive intense concentration practice known as the four dignities. They are walking, being, sitting, and lying. *Unsui* are sincere Dharma seekers, but they are also funny and brisk.

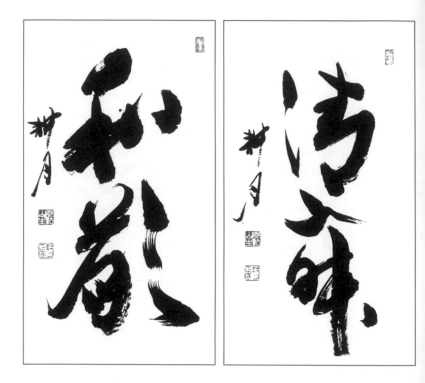

Harmony, reverence, purity, tranquillity
Wa Kei Sei Jaku

These four elements are traditionally said to be the essential spirit of the art of tea.

Wa means "harmony" or "tenderness." When Master Dōgen, after years of practice, came back from China to Japan, people thought that he had brought many precious things with him. They asked, "What did you get in China and what did you bring back?" Dōgen replied, "I came back with empty hands. I learned only some degree of tenderness."

Kei means "reverence." Our zazen practice breaks our old notions and changes our attitudes from carelessness to carefulness. Instead of taking things for granted, the spirit of gratitude grows. Reverential acts can only come from gratitude to inanimate as well as animate beings.

When such a humble spirit is born, our hearts become pure, and that is *sei.*

The final word, *jaku,* is *nirvāna* in Sanskrit, which means "extinction." To translate it as "tranquillity" is not adequate. Nirvana is self-realization, insight from which harmony, reverence, and purity come.

Therefore, the spiritual order of the four elements should be *jaku, sei, kei, wa.*

Mountain is mountain, water is water

Yama Kore Yama, Mizu Kore Mizu

When an American professor who taught philosophy at a university heard this famous Zen saying, he reacted with a negative attitude. However, other elements of Zen strongly attracted him, so he went to Japan and met a Zen master who explained, "At first, mountain is mountain, water is water. As a second step, mountain is not mountain, water is not water," the master continued. "As a third step, mountain is mountain, water is water."

The American professor asked, "What's the difference between the first step and the third step?" The Zen master said, "At first, mountain is mountain and water is water." Of the third step, he said with the loudest possible voice, "MOUNTAIN *IS* MOUNTAIN, WATER *IS* WATER!" With this, the professor got some insight.

From an unenlightened viewpoint, mountain is mountain, water is water; from an enlightened viewpoint, a mountain is also a mountain, water is also water. However, there is a hidden spiritual journey in the enlightened viewpoint; that is the period of mountain is not mountain, water is not water. The negation "not" is what we call practice.

Willow is green, flower is red
Yanagi Wa Midori Hana Wa Kurenai

One of the most profound statements in the Buddhist tradition is, "Things are not what they seem, nor are they otherwise." Or sometimes they say, "thusness" or "as-it-isness."

> Willow is green—thusness
> Flower is red—as-it-isness

If that is all, it may be too simple. Green willow is not what it seems. Yet, after all, green willow is nothing but just green willow.

During the eleventh century in China, there was a distinguished poet called Sotoba, who said, "The willow is green, flower is red; they are the true masters of themselves," and he added, "The simplicity is the breathtaking reality."

In order to see true greenness, true redness, we must experience a spiritual transformation; that is to say, we must pass through the denial period of willow is not willow, red is not red. Then we can truly appreciate the shining greenness of willow, the sparkling redness of flower.

A modern Japanese haiku poet, Santōka (1882–1940), wrote, "Westerners like to conquer mountains; Orientals like to contemplate them. As for me, I like to taste the mountains."

Snowflakes do not fall
on an inappropriate place

Yuki Bessho Ni Ochizu

There was a Zen layman, Hō (d. 808), in China. One winter day he visited Master Yakusan (751–834). A few monks saw him off. At the temple gate, Hō said, "What beautiful snowflakes—each one of them does not fall on another's place." One of the monks asked, "Where do they fall?" Hō slapped at the monk's cheek as though saying, "Here!"

This is the origin of this phrase, but, again, we must not be deluded by the word "snow"; whatever it may be—wind blowing, man smiling, dog barking—it is appropriate at that moment and for that circumstance.

Life and death are exactly like that. There is nothing particularly depressing—depression is just depression, nothing else. There is nothing particularly exciting—excitement is just excitement, nothing else. There is nothing particularly sad about passing away—passing away is just passing away, nothing else.

Dream

Yume

In the *Diamond Sūtra* there is a well-known verse that goes:

> All composite things
> Are like a dream, a fantasy, a bubble, and a shadow,
> Are like a dewdrop and a flash of lightning.
> They are *thus* to be regarded.

This verse speaks not only about what we consider composite things but also about such things as life and the cosmos; in fact, everything is like a dream that has no fixed entity—śūnyatā. The dream also implies impermanency, one of the essential teachings of Buddhism.

Thus "Dream" is the condensed expression of *śūnyatā* and impermanency—the quintessence of Buddha Dharma.

Wherever you are,
you are the Master

Zuisho Ni Shu To Naru

This is an extremely well known saying by Master Rinzai, which means: Wherever you stand, that place is the very place of reality. Perhaps it is more comprehensible if it is stated in a different way: When you are with it, you are your own Master.

From the *honbun* (fundamental) point of view, whether we are with it or not, we cannot be anything else but our own true Master. However, from the *shusho* (existential) point of view, we need the practice of mindfulness. We must be "with it," and we need self-realization to understand that whether we are with it or not, we cannot be anything *but* Master.

Index

About the Author and the Illustrator

Eidō Tai Shimano practiced Zen under the guidance of the late Sōen Nakagawa Rōshi and became his succesor. He is now the president of the Zen Studies Society and abbot of the New York Zendō Shōbō-ji, both in New York City, and abbot of Dai Bosatsu Zendō Kongō-ji in Upstate New York. He is the author of *Points of Departure: Zen Buddhism with a Rinzai View.*

Kōgetsu Tani studied at Buddhist University in Kyoto and, until his death in 1994, was abbot of Shōgen-ji and president of Shōgen Junior College in Japan.